BRITISH BUSES AND COACHES IN THE 1960s

A PANORAMIC VIEW

BRITISH BUSES AND COACHES IN THE 1960s

A PANORAMIC VIEW

JIM BLAKE

PEN & SWORD
TRANSPORT

AN IMPRINT OF PEN & SWORD BOOKS LTD.
YORKSHIRE - PHILADELPHIA

First published in Great Britain in 2021 by
Pen and Sword Transport
An imprint of
Pen & Sword Books Ltd.
Yorkshire - Philadelphia

ISBN 978 1 47386 781 9

Typeset by SJmagic DESIGN SERVICES, India.

Printed and bound in India by Replika Press Pvt. Ltd.

Pen & Sword Books Ltd incorporates the Imprints of Pen & Sword Books Archaeology, Atlas, Aviation, Battleground, Discovery, Family History, History, Maritime, Military, Naval, Politics, Railways, Select, Transport, True Crime, Fiction, Frontline Books, Leo Cooper, Praetorian Press, Seaforth Publishing, Wharncliffe and White Owl.

For a complete list of Pen & Sword titles please contact

PEN & SWORD BOOKS LIMITED
47 Church Street, Barnsley, South Yorkshire, S70 2AS, England
E-mail: enquiries@pen-and-sword.co.uk
Website: www.pen-and-sword.co.uk

or

PEN AND SWORD BOOKS
1950 Lawrence Rd, Havertown, PA 19083, USA
E-mail: Uspen-and-sword@casematepublishers.com
Website: www.penandswordbooks.com

CONTENTS

Introduction *6*

Pictures 7

About the Author *190*

INTRODUCTION

Following on from the recent volumes of photographs from my archives of buses, coaches and trolleybuses in various categories of operator I have produced for Pen & Sword Books, I have now been asked to come up with another one, featuring them from all types of operator. This I am delighted to do, since there are lots, lots more where they came from!

Owing to the sheer volume of material I have available, it has been necessary to split this into two separate volumes, one featuring London Transport, and the other featuring other bus and coach operators up and down the country.

This volume deals with the latter, and therefore the 300 or so photographs included show a tremendous variety of bus and coach types, some old and some new. All were taken on my travels throughout the 1960s, and I am indebted to the PSV Circle and to the Ian Allan 'ABC booklets' for providing most of the basic details of the vehicles concerned, much of which, however, I also noted at the time I saw them.

Thanks also go to friends such as Ken Wright, Paul Everett and Steve Newman for helping fill in various details I could not find from these sources, and to Colin Clarke and John Scott-Morgan without whom I could never have put this book together. Particularly from the spring of 1965 onwards, I was out and about almost every weekend on day trips to various parts of the country, either travelling by train to such places as Birmingham, Manchester, Liverpool or Nottingham with a couple of friends, or on organised trips by enthusiasts' groups such as the Omnibus Society, the PSV Circle and the Omnibus Tourist Circle. I must pass on my thanks to such people as John Kaye, Alan Osborne, the late George Ledger and Martin Haywood who organised such trips 55 or 60 or so years ago and therefore made it possible for me to take many of the photographs included herein. The vast majority of the pictures in this book have never been published before.

JIM BLAKE
Palmers Green
June 2021

One of the best-known British independent bus and coach fleets was Barton of Chilwell, Nottinghamshire. Here, their No.739 is one of two of their vehicles seen at Peterborough Bus Station on Easter Sunday, 22 April 1962. It is a 1948 Leyland Tiger PS1/B which was rebodied as a lowbridge double-decker by Willowbrook in 1956, seating 61. It is working a service that had recently been taken over from Cream Bus Services.

This unfortunately rather blurred shot shows vehicles typical of the East Kent Road Car Company at their Canterbury depot on 3 August 1962. Nearest the camera is 1949 lowbridge Guy Arab III EFN200, which accompanies two Dennis Lancet J3s of similar vintage, one in original half-cab condition, the other rebuilt with a full front to allow one-man operation. All have Park Royal bodywork.

Particularly following the drastic service cuts of 1958, many London Transport RT-type buses found new homes with other British operators when they became surplus to LT's requirements. This one is former RT420, sold initially to Brown's Blue Buses of Leicester in 1958 but now operating for Super Coaches of Upminster. It is seen alongside former RTL20 at King's Cross Coach Station on 23 April 1963. Note how it has been fitted with platform doors. Despite this, it was scrapped in 1965.

Seen at Victoria Coach Station on 26 April 1963, 543EYL is a brand new AEC Reliance with Duple Northern Alpine coachwork, built to the recently newly-permitted length of 36ft. It belongs to Timpsons of Catford and accompanies a United Counties ECW-bodied Bristol MW.

Another new 36ft-long Reliance there that day is Aldershot & District No.480, which has Park Royal 49-seat coachwork.

Two older coaches present are Midland Red Nos.4213 and 4210 which were built in 1954 with Willowbrook 37-seat coachwork on the company's own type C3 chassis. This company was well-known for building its own buses and coaches for many years.

With its chassis and bodywork also built by the company, Midland Red No.5065 is a class S15 44-seat single-decker built in 1962, which has also worked to Victoria on Easter Bank Holiday relief duty.

The Burlingham Seagull was one of the most popular coach designs of the mid/late 1950s. This example is a Leyland Tiger Cub built in 1958, No.4 in the fleet of Ribble subsidiary Standerwick. Note also the adverts on the wall behind it for various operators serving the coach station.

In the main Ribble fleet, No.1019 is a 1961 Leyland Leopard L2 with Harrington Cavalier coachwork, seating only 28 and used on luxury tours. On 29 May 1963, it has brought a party to the Epsom Derby and is seen afterwards at Victoria Coach Station.

Whitsun 1963 brought a number of unscheduled vehicles working reliefs to Victoria Coach Station. One is Wilts & Dorset 1956 ECW-bodied Bristol LS5G No.548 on hire to Royal Blue, seen on 31 May 1963.

Each year between 1959 and 1965, I spent a fortnight's holiday with my parents at Swalecliffe, and therefore became very familiar with, and fond of, East Kent's buses and coaches in their striking maroon and cream livery. Here at Folkestone Bus Station on 31 July 1963 is their YJG825, an AEC Regent V with Park Royal 72-seat highbridge forward-entrance bodywork new in 1962. Batches of this type were delivered to them in 1961, 1962, 1963, 1964, 1966 and 1967. Fortunately, some survive today in preservation, along with some of the full-fronted versions new in 1959.

In contrast to the Regent V seen earlier, CJG981 is a lowbridge all-Leyland Titan PD1 53-seater, new in 1947 and now one of the oldest buses in the fleet. This view also shows the substantial bus shelters built at Folkestone Bus Station, a far cry from the flimsy structures more common nowadays.

A pre-war vehicle retained by East Kent at this period is JG9937, a Park Royal-bodied Leyland Tiger TS8 coach new in 1938. It is in use at Folkestone Harbour as a booking office for day trips to France. Note the publicity for these, emphasising that no passports are needed.

Recently withdrawn by East Kent, JG7016 was the last pre-war Leyland Titan TD4 in stock. Rebodied as a 53-seat lowbridge bus after the war, it accompanies wartime utility Guy Arab I BJG304, now used as a tree-lopper, in the yard of Herne Bay depot on 1 August 1963. Both have Park Royal bodies.

It was common practice in the 1950s and early 1960s for old buses and coaches to be used as living accommodation for showmen operating travelling fairgrounds. Their engines were also often used to power generators to work merry-go-rounds and so on. An ancient example of this seen at Hampstead Heath fair on 30 March 1964 is RX4352, a Leyland Titan TD1 that had been new to Thames Valley in 1929.

During the winter of 1963/64, most of London Transport's private hire RF class coaches were withdrawn. Several were purchased by the famous Cambridgeshire independent bus and coach operator Premier Travel. On 10 May 1964, three of them – former RF9, 6 and 7 and now Nos. 167, 164 and 165 – pose outside this operator's Chrishall depot for an Omnibus Society visit.

Once a common type in Premier Travel's fleet, No.113 (KGY940) is a 1949 Dennis Lancet J3 with Park Royal 33-seat coachwork. It now awaits disposal at their West Wratting depot.

At Premier Travel's Haverhill depot, their No.127 is an early post-war Bristol K5G with standard ECW 55-seat lowbridge bodywork, recently acquired from West Yorkshire.

Another early post-war Bristol/ECW product is Western National LWL6B 37-seat coach No.1316, which has just arrived at Victoria Coach Station on Royal Blue relief duty on 16 May 1964.

Also at Victoria that day, Scottish Omnibuses' B103A is a brand new AEC Reliance 41-seater with Alexander coachwork typical of the type being supplied to Scottish Bus Group fleets. This bodywork was also by now becoming popular with fleets south of the border, too.

A day trip to Southend on 18 May 1964 finds the Corporation's 1960 Park Royal-bodied AEC Bridgemaster No.317 outside Southend Victoria station. This 30ft-long lowheight double-decker seated no fewer than 76 passengers!

Also at Southend Victoria, the Corporation's No.310 is more typical of their fleet, being a lowbridge Massey-bodied Leyland Titan PD2/40 55-seater, new in 1957.

At Ryde Esplanade on 28 May 1964 is Southern Vectis No.846, a recently delivered Bristol SUL4A with ECW 36-seat bodywork.

The London County Council, by whom I was now employed at their County Hall headquarters, had a large fleet of school buses. Many had unusual bodywork, including VXM870, a Morris 3K with an Appleyard body, new in 1958. It is seen at their Greenwich depot on 27 February 1965. The Council's traditional dark green livery will be replaced by light blue and white when these vehicles transfer to the new Inner London Education Authority on 1 April 1965.

Another unusual body is this early post-war Yeates full-fronted 37-seater on a Dennis Lancet J10C chassis. NBH856 is in the fleet of Canham of Whittlesea, and seen in Midland Road, St. Pancras, on 6 March 1965.

Once I was earning my own living, at the princely sum of £515 per annum, I was able to travel further afield to visit bus and coach operators. The very first visit I made to the Midlands was to Leicester on 14 March 1965. This is the City Corporation's No.90, a Leyland Titan PD3/1 with East Lancs 74-seat bodywork, new in 1958.

A much older Leicester City Transport bus in service that day is their No.5, a 1948 AEC Regent III with Birmingham-style MCCW 60-seat bodywork. It is followed by a much newer Leyland Titan PD3/1 and also bears the Corporation's earlier livery of maroon and cream.

Sporting events at Wembley in the mid-1960s always brought a wide range of interesting buses and coaches. On 3 April 1965, for the schoolboys' international football match, a very unusual bus to be seen in the London area is DJY965, a Crossley-bodied DD42/7 that had been new in 1948 as Plymouth Corporation No.335 and is now with Wesley's Coaches of Stoke Goldington.

The 120 Cravens-bodied RTs delivered to London Transport in 1948/49/50 were non-standard and therefore withdrawn and sold in 1956/57. After that, they were not often seen in London, although one or two were actually owned by independent fleets in the London area. One was former RT1462 (KGK721) which worked for Linkline Coaches of Harlesden for a few months in 1965. It is seen here in Victoria on Good Friday, 16 April 1965, having taken a party of churchgoers to nearby Westminster Cathedral for a memorial service to Mother Maria Skobstkova.

Shamrock & Rambler was a well-known Bournemouth-based independent coach operator. Also at Victoria on Easter Saturday, 17 April 1965, 1955-built REL56 is the last Duple Vega-bodied Bedford SBO in its fleet and is on hire to Royal Blue. Shamrock & Rambler was taken over by the Transport Holding Company Ltd (Tilling Group) in 1966.

A trip to Maidstone on 30 April 1965 finds Maidstone & District DH162, a 1945 Bristol K6A which originally had a wartime utility body but was given a new Weymann Orion 56-seat body in 1954, still in service at Lower Stone Street bus station. It is now due for early withdrawal.

Two other rebodied wartime Maidstone & District double-deckers which have been withdrawn are DH75 and DH78. They are 1944 Guy Arab Is with Weymann 56-bodies, new in 1952, and are now painted grey and awaiting disposal in the yard of Chatham depot.

For the 1965 FA Cup Final on 1 May, many Wallace Arnold of Leeds coaches brought Leeds United supporters to see their team play Liverpool. One such was 1961 Duple Super Vega-bodied Thames Trader 9930UG, in the livery of subsidiary Kitchin Coaches. Its passengers must have gone home disappointed: Liverpool won 2-1.

A very odd vehicle is 150AOU, which has an AEC Regent III chassis built in 1954, but was used experimentally by its manufacturer until 1959, when it was given a Roe lowbridge full-front, forward entrance 56-seat body and sold to Liss & District. It is seen here on 15 May 1965 parked at Lincoln's Inn Fields, by now working a private hire for Super of Upminster.

Thurgood-bodied Bedford SB3 coaches were once a familiar sight with London sightseeing operator Evan Evans Tours, but by 21 May 1965, WXE942, which dates from 1959, was one of only three remaining. It is picking up sightseers outside Westminster Abbey.

Seen in Waterloo Road coach park, BBV931 is something of an oddity, being an AEC Regal III new in 1948 to Ribblesdale Coaches and subsequently given a new Yeates Europa 37-seat full-front body. It is owned by Everson of Wix when seen here.

Awaiting departure for Clacton and Jaywick Sands at the doomed King's Cross coach station is Sutton of Clacton's VVW531, a 1952 Leyland Royal Tiger with Duple 41-seat coachwork. This coach station, on the corner of Pentonville Road and Northdown Street, was closed a few months later and the site built on for office development.

A trip to Oxford on 9 June 1965 finds City of Oxford Motor Services' 1951 Weymann-bodied AEC Regent III highbridge 56-seater No.916 entering their Cowley Road depot. This was now one of the oldest buses in their fleet.

In the City's bus station, No.188 is a Weymann-bodied 56-seat lowbridge AEC Regent V dating from 1956. It is noteworthy that it retains a Regent III-style radiator.

Typical of City of Oxford Motor Services' single-deckers is No.795, a 44-seat Willowbrook-bodied AEC Reliance built in 1964.

Loading up opposite the Regal cinema in Cowley Road is City of Oxford's No.312, a 72-seat Park Royal-bodied AEC Bridgemaster new in 1962.

A regular visitor to Waterloo Road coach park at this period is Alexander Midland MPD224, a 1963 Leyland Tiger Cub with prototype Alexander 38-seat coachwork. As its blind shows, it is on a tour from Scotland to London and Bournemouth.

It was a typical sight at this period to see queues of coaches along Buckingham Palace Road waiting to enter Victoria Coach Station, as Grey Cars' TCC847 is doing when on hire to Royal Blue on 3 July 1965. It is a Beadle-Commer integral coach, new in 1957 to this coaching arm of Devon General.

I made my first of many trips to Birmingham on 4 July 1965. As well as north London, Birmingham also has a suburb called Highgate, complete with a former tram depot in Highgate Road! This is the location of Birmingham City Transport No.1930, a 1948 Daimler CVG6 with MCCW 54-seat bodywork, seen on the Corporation's famous No.8 Inner Circle route. Buses of this batch were now being withdrawn.

At Snow Hill in the city centre, new office blocks rise in the background as 1954 Crossley-bodied Daimler CVG6 55-seater No.3164 calls on route 72 to Handsworth. This was one of the last batch of half-cab double-deckers supplied to the Corporation, totalling 125 vehicles in all.

Birmingham's Selly Oak garage has many Crossley-bodied DD42/7s with typical Birmingham-style 55-seat bodies. Seen at the rear of that garage, No.2415 dates from 1950.

Daimler CVD6
No.1967 dates from 1949 and awaits disposal at the rear of the garage, one of 100 built that year with MCCW 54-seat bodywork.

Also in Birmingham that day, and seen at Digbeth, Western SMT IT1267 is an unusual combination – a 1957 Bristol LS6G with Alexander coachwork. Because the Scottish Bus Group was nationalised, but not tied to buying only Bristol and ECW products, such combinations were permissible.

I spent my last summer holiday at Swalecliffe in 1965, and here at Canterbury Bus Station on 28 July 1965, East Kent 1947 all-Leyland Titan PD1 lowbridge 53-seater CJG983 stands with a variety of the operator's other buses. It is now one of the last survivors of its batch, and is working a rush hour relief duty on route 17.

At Canterbury that day too is East Kent FFN450, a Park Royal-bodied 39-seat Leyland Royal Tiger touring coach, new in 1951.

Also on rush hour relief duties is East Kent EFN181, one of a batch of Guy Arab IIIs with Park Royal 53-seat lowbridge bodywork, new in 1950.

CJG947, another surviving 1947 all-Leyland PD1, arrives at Canterbury Bus Station. What route it is working is unclear by its blind display.

Another elderly East Kent coach seen at Canterbury that day is GFN271, one of a number of Beadle-bodied vehicles constructed integrally in 1952 using parts from pre-war Leyland Titan TD5 double-deckers. This one has been reinstated for the 1965 summer season, which will be its last.

The bus station has emptied out somewhat by the time I took this shot of CFN126, one of East Kent's 1948 Dennis Lancet J3s whose Park Royal bodies were modified in 1959 with full fronts and forward entrances, to permit one-man operation. Three of the fleet's famous AEC Regent Vs complete the picture, the one in the centre being of the 1959 full-fronted PFN batch.

Seen on the seafront at Herne Bay when operating an excursion on 1 August 1965 is East Kent HJG3, a Dennis Lancet LUF with 41-seat Duple coachwork, new in 1954.

On 3 August 1965 another surviving East Kent 1947 all-Leyland PD1, CJG982, accompanies Park Royal-bodied Royal Tiger coach FFN449 at Folkestone Harbour.

Two more of this batch, CJG981 and CJG983, await rush hour relief duties in Folkestone Bus Station.

At East Kent's Cheriton depot is CFN133, another of the rebuilt 1948 Park Royal-bodied Dennis Lancet J3 35-seaters.

A last look at one of the all-Leyland Titan PD1s, CJG977, which is nicely blinded up for local route 99 at Cheriton depot.

Also at Folkestone that day are two AEC Reliances belonging to the famous Leeds coach company Wallace Arnold, 9205NW and 9199NW. Although both date from 1959 and have Plaxton bodywork, the latter has an earlier body style.

An oddity seen on 8 August 1965 under the trolleybus wires near Trent Bridge is Nottingham City Transport No.812, a pre-war AEC Regal retained for use as a staff canteen. The structure on its roof is a water tank to keep the cups of tea going!

A visit to Coventry on 15 August 1965 finds these 1949 Daimler CVA6s, with MCCW 60-seat bodywork, at the Corporation's Hartnall Lane depot. They are now only used in rush hours, and are being withdrawn. Nos. 60, 50 and 96 are nearest the camera.

Also at Hartnall Lane, Nos. 150 and 136 are 58-seat MCCW-bodied Daimler CVD6 58-seaters, new in 1951/52. By now, these are only used on weekdays.

On 22 August 1965, I visited Birmingham again. At the Corporation's Cotteridge garage, No.3031 is a Guy Arab IV with 55-seat MCCW bodywork dating from 1954. This is built to the standard Birmingham 'tin-front' design of the period.

I was also in Birmingham the following Sunday, 29 August 1965. Here, 1949 Crossley-bodied DD42/4 54-seater No.2383 is with a batch of withdrawn vehicles awaiting disposal outside Washwood Heath garage. Stripped of its engine, it appears to have suffered rear-end damage. Next to it is Daimler CVD6 No.1987, also dating from 1949 but with similar MCCW bodywork.

No.1884, a 1949 Daimler CVG6 with MCCW 54-seat bodywork, appears to have been withdrawn owing to accident damage, but unlike most of the other condemned buses, has not had its engine removed.

A visit to Colchester Bus Station on 7 September 1965 finds ACF181, a 1948 Thurgood-bodied Bedford OB 29-seater new to Norfolk's of Nayland, one of the many independent bus operators that worked into the town. It is dwarfed by an elderly Eastern National Bristol K5G.

A trip to Southampton on 19 September 1965 finds their 1949 Park Royal-bodied Guy Arab III 65-seater No.197 changing crew outside the Corporation's Shirley depot. This was typical of a large fleet of these buses operated by them.

One of the oldest buses still in use with a municipal operator in 1965 is Eastbourne Corporation No.12, an all-Leyland Lion LT9 32-seater new in 1939. It is seen outside their depot, posed for an Omnibus Society visit on 26 September 1965. Behind is No.11, an East Lancs-bodied AEC Regal III 30-seater new in 1950, and also by now a rarity. Both have since been preserved.

On 3 October 1965, I was in the Midlands yet again, this time visiting Barton's Chilwell headquarters. Recently withdrawn there is their No.858, a 1946 Massey-bodied Leyland Titan PD1 56-seater acquired from Birkenhead Corporation in 1960.

Also withdrawn at Chilwell are No.875, a 1946 all-Leyland Titan PD1 lowbridge 53-seater acquired from Preston Corporation in 1960, and No.430. The latter was new to Barton in 1942, and is a Guy Arab I still with its original Northern Counties utility 55-seat lowbridge body.

In common with many other operators, Barton often converted withdrawn buses to towing wagons. This has happened to No.609, a Roe-bodied Leyland Titan TD5 double-decker that had been new to West Riding in 1938. It accompanies 1960 Duple-bodied Bedford C5Z1 dual-purpose 29-seat coach No.935, acquired from Robin Hood Coaches in 1961.

Another well-known independent bus fleet was King Alfred of Winchester. Here, on 9 October 1965, their EHO181 is a wartime Guy Arab II with utility bodywork which has been cut down for use as a tree-lopper. It stands outside the disused Chesil station, near to their depot.

Typical of King Alfred's fleet at the time is JOR593. This is a 1951 all-Leyland Titan PD2/2 highbridge 56-seater, whose upper deck has been rebuilt by Reading in 1964 following a low bridge accident.

Grey Green
Coaches, and its subsidiaries Orange Luxury Coaches and Fallowfield & Britten, were one of London's best-known coaching firms, operating coastal express services, excursions, tours and private hires. At their Stamford Hill headquarters on 16 December 1965, YXA364 is a 1960 Bedford SB8 with Harrington Crusader 37-seat coachwork. Lighter coaches like this were used for private hire and tours work, and usually replaced after four years. However, this one and several others have been retained for use on London Transport's Drayton Park to Finsbury Park shuttle service, replacing the Northern City Line tube service.

At Wembley on 12 March 1966 for an international Hockey match, LYH93 is a 1951 Harrington-bodied Leyland Royal Tiger, new to Grey Green subsidiary Fallowfield & Britten, but now operated by Jennings Coaches of Camberwell.

Reliance of Newbury was an independent bus and coach operator, who operated local services around the town as well as school and industrial contracts. Somewhat unusual for such a fleet is their No.75, a 1954 Bedford SBO with Duple Midland 40-seat bodywork, acquired from Corvedale of Ludlow in 1960. It is seen in Newbury Bus Station on 26 March 1966.

At Reliance's depot the same day is No.81, an elderly AEC Regal II with Duple 35-seat coachwork, new in 1946 and acquired by them only in 1962.

Also at Newbury Bus Station is Thames Valley No.525, a 1950 Bristol K6B with standard ECW 55-seat lowbridge bodywork. One of the oldest buses in their fleet, it has recently been reinstated.

My first trip to the Midlands in 1966 was to Birmingham on Easter Sunday, 10 April 1966. Typical of the Corporation's newer buses is No.3316, an MCW-bodied Daimler Fleetline, new in 1963. It is seen at the famous Bull Ring.

Another vehicle from Birmingham is seen arriving at Wembley Stadium for the schoolboys' international football match on 30 April 1966. This is Gliderways' 1959 Harrington Wayfarer-bodied Leyland Tiger Cub 718FHA.

Also at Wembley are Midland General 1965 Bristol MW6G No.213, with ECW 41-seat dual-purpose bodywork, and NEW790, a 1955 AEC Reliance with rare Roe Dalesman coachwork belonging to Ouse Valley Coaches.

Illustrating how coaches of all shapes and sizes brought spectators to Wembley Stadium is HTM20, an early post-war Bedford OB with Duple Vista 29-seat coachwork. It is operated by Bailey's Coaches of Turvey, near Bedford.

Typical of mid-1950s ECW-bodied Bristol coaches in Tilling Group fleets is Eastern National No.327, a 1957 LS6B 39-seater. Allocated to Brentwood depot, it had originally been in the associated fleet of Thomas Tilling, based at King's Cross.

From not far away is Harold Wood Coaches 3314F, a 1956 Commer TS3 integral with Beadle 'Rochester' coachwork, which is actually on hire to Eastern National to take youngsters to Wembley.

A pouring wet Sunday, 8 May 1966, finds two elderly Bristol Omnibus Company (BOC) Bristol L5G rear-entrance 35-seaters with the inevitable ECW bodywork. Seen at their Lawrence Hill depot and works, they date from 1949 and are two of the last survivors of this type in service with BOC. Two newer Bristol/ECW coaches may be seen in the distance.

The following Sunday, 15 May 1966, I visited Eastern Coachworks' (ECW) factory at Lowestoft. Amongst standard ECW-bodied Bristol buses and coaches awaiting delivery are Central SMT BL327, an FLF Lodekka with 76-seat bodywork, and Crosville CMG570, a 39-seat MW6G coach. Note the unusual blind boxes on the Scottish Lodekkas.

On the same day in Ipswich, 1950 Park Royal-bodied AEC Regent III 56-seater No.1 was the Corporation's very first motor bus, since hitherto they had operated only trams and trolleybuses. It is seen outside their Constantine Road depot. The vehicle behind is similar Regent III No.17, dating from 1956.

Another visit to Birmingham on 22 May 1966 sees the Corporation's No.2238, a 1950 MCCW-bodied Leyland Tiger PS2 34-seater, outside Selly Oak garage in the company of one of their 1950 Leyland Olympics (also MCCW-bodied) and one of their odd Marshall-bodied single-deck Daimler Fleetlines, new in 1965.

On the same day, Midland Red class S10 single-deck 44-seater No.3635 also dates from 1950 and is seen at their Edgbaston Works. These buses were some of the earliest British underfloor-engined single-deckers and had either Brush or MCCW bodywork to Midland Red's design. This one is now being used for road tests.

Another of Midland Red's self-built buses at Edgbaston is 1950 D5B No.3828, which is now awaiting disposal. Brush supplied the Midland Red-designed bodies for the hundred 56-seat buses of this class.

Seen in its last season of service, XMT329 is a 1952 Duple Vega-bodied SB, one of many in the fleet of Garner's Coaches of Hounslow. It is at Wembley for the Rugby Cup Final on 21 May 1966.

Quite an oddity at Wembley that day is DMS517, an elderly AEC Regal III with very rare Brockhouse full-fronted 37-seat coachwork and now owned by a scout group.

Also at Wembley is YXH865, a very smart Plaxton-bodied AEC Reliance 41-seater new in 1959 to London coach operator Frames Tours Ltd.

Completion of
the electrification of the West Coast Main Line between Euston, Liverpool and Manchester enabled me to visit the latter city for a day for the first time on 29 May 1966. Seen near Piccadilly is CCN429, a Weymann-bodied Guy Arab III that had been new to Northern General in 1952 as their No.1429 and had recently been sold. Behind it is one of the North Western Road Car Company's recent lowbridge Alexander-bodied Daimler Fleetlines.

Typical of
Manchester City Transport's older double-deckers is No.3281, an all-Leyland 58-seater Titan PD2/3, new in 1950 and seen under the trolleybus wires at Piccadilly.

Contrasting with the red and cream livery of Manchester City Transport's buses, those from Ashton-Under-Lyne were also seen in the city centre – No.43, a 1965 Roe-bodied Leyland Titan PD2/40 65-seater, new in 1965, carries a blue and cream livery and is seen at Lower Mosley Street. Buses in Salford's dark green and cream, Bury's light green and cream, Bolton's and Oldham's maroon and cream, Stalybridge's green, and Stockport's red and cream could also be seen. All would be taken over a few years later by the South East Lancs and North East Cheshire PTE (SELNEC for short).

Back in London on 31 May 1966, Southdown 1951 Harrington-bodied Leyland Royal Tiger PSU1/16 41-seat coach No.1689 is seen at Victoria Coach Station when on loan to fellow BET operator Aldershot & District in its final season of service prior to withdrawal.

A well-known independent bus operator based in Aylesbury was Red Rover, a subsidiary of Keith Coaches. Many of their vehicles were ex-London RT types, but there were also some newer vehicles, notably JPP11C, a 1965 AEC Reliance with Marshall 53-seat bodywork. It was in fact their newest vehicle when seen at their depot on 4 June 1966.

In contrast, Red Rover RR2 is one of the non-standard Craven RTs that had been sold by London Transport in 1956/57. It was originally RT1519, and was withdrawn at the end of 1966, having spent some ten years with Red Rover as opposed to some six and a half with LT!

A visit to United Counties on 19 June 1966 finds two of their typical Bristol/ECW buses outside their Northampton depot: 1954 L5G 45-seater No.454 and 1949 K5G lowbridge 55-seater No.800.

Inside United Counties' Kettering depot are two of their elderly Bristol L-type single-deckers. No.403 on the left is an LWL5G 39-seater, new in 1951 and recently withdrawn, whilst KNO602 is a 1946 L5G 35-seater acquired from Eastern National, originally No.303 in United Counties' fleet, and demoted to training duties following withdrawal in 1961.

A more recent United Counties vehicle is No.678, a 1965 FS6B 60-seater specially painted in cream livery to commemorate the 800th anniversary of Bedford being granted its charter. It is posed for members of an Omnibus Society tour at Bedford depot.

An oddity seen at Nottingham's Broad Marsh Bus Station on 26 June 1966 is DRN344, a 1951 Sentinel STC6 that had been new to Ribble as their No.287, and is now a mobile cafe.

At Nottingham's Huntingdon Street Bus Station on the same day are two elderly Barton vehicles – No.465, one of their unique Duple forward-entrance Leyland Titan PD1s, dating from 1947 and seating 55, and No.724, a 1954 BTS1 rebuild with Plaxton 39-seat coachwork.

Barton No.573 is another of the Duple-bodied PD1s, this time of the 1948 batch, and is seen at Mount Street, Nottingham.

During this period, there was an overtime ban by London Transport Central Area operating staff, so any special service LT operated had to be contracted out to other operators. On 2 July 1966, Valliant of Ealing's 1956 Duple-bodied AEC Reliance 41-seater SXC116 is seen on hire to LT outside Wimbledon Station, operating the special service to and from the tennis tournament. It had recently been acquired from the Royal Arsenal Co-operative Society, Woolwich, to whom it was new.

A trip to Derby next day, 3 July 1966, finds the Corporation's No.104, a Daimler CVD6 with Willowbrook/Brush 56-seat bodywork, outside their Park Gates depot.

Still in the livery of its original owner, the Yorkshire independent Hanson, their former No. 348 (MCX386) has in fact recently been sold to east London operator Silvertown Coaches. It is a Plaxton-bodied Bedford SBG 41-seater, new in 1957, and is seen arriving at Wembley Stadium for the World Cup match between England and Uruguay, on 11 July 1966.

Another trip to Manchester on 16 July 1966 finds Manchester City Transport No.3254, a Leyland Titan PD2/3 with MCCW bodywork, new in 1951 and part of a batch of 100, the last 35 of which had Leyland-built bodies. This type of body was to the Corporation's own specification and was also built by other manufacturers.

With an electrically hauled express from Manchester Piccadilly to London Euston in the background, Manchester 1947 Crossley DD42/4 No.2072, with Crossley bodywork in the same style, awaits disposal at Hyde Road. What a shame electric traction on Manchester's streets is soon to be abandoned, as evidenced by two withdrawn trolleybuses dating only from 1955, with No.1349 nearest the camera.

Oldham Corporation also worked into Manchester City Centre. Their No.350 is a 1949 Leyland Titan PD2/3 with Roe 56-seat bodywork, seen setting off for home.

At Oldham Corporation's depot, No.250 is a Leyland Titan PD1/3 dating from 1947, also with Roe bodywork, and it appears the worse for wear, whilst next to it, 1946 PD1 No.239 is most definitely kaput! The notice in its windscreen is a prohibition from the Ministry of Transport against it being used. Shortly before my visit here, the men from the ministry had descended on the Corporation's depot and declared many of their buses as being unfit for service. This resulted from a very lax maintenance regime, under which some buses had not had a major overhaul for 10 years or more!

In contrast, Ashton-Under-Lyne Corporation's buses were kept in smart condition. Their No.65, a Bond-bodied Guy Arab IV new in 1956, is out of use at their depot, having an engine overhaul.

SHMD half-cab single-decker No.103 looks a lot older than it really is, being a Northern Counties 35-seat rear-entrance Daimler CVD6, one of five delivered with this style of bodywork in 1950. It is seen in Ashton-Under-Lyne bus station. This operator had a number of quaint vehicles, to match its quaint name, which was Stalybridge, Hyde, Mossley and Dunkinfield Transport & Electricity Board!

A visitor to Manchester on 16 July 1966 is Central SMT AC3, a brand new Albion Viking with Alexander dual-purpose 40-seat bodywork. It is on hire to Western SMT for their Glasgow to Manchester express service, and is seen outside Manchester Exchange station.

At Wembley on 23 July 1966 is South Wales independent operator Jones of Aberbeeg's VAX578, a Leyland Tiger Cub with Duple Britannia coachwork, new in 1959. The occasion was one of the quarter finals of the World Cup, in which England beat Argentina 1-0.

An Omnibus Touring Circle trip next day, 24 July 1966, to various operators in Gloucestershire, finds Kearsey of Cheltenham 1955 Burlingham-bodied AEC Reliance 44-seater No.73 (ODG982) picking up passengers in its home town.

The main operator in Cheltenham on this day is Bristol Omnibus Company subsidiary Cheltenham District. Here, No.78, one of two remaining Duple-bodied Guy Arab III 57-seaters, new in 1950, is seen at their depot.

One of hundreds of coaches at Wembley for the World Cup Final on 30 July 1966, in which England beat West Germany 4-2, is Southdown No.1058, a Beadle-bodied Leyland Tiger Cub, new in 1956 and now in its last season of service with them.

A stranger in town later that day is Alexander Midland MPD274, a 41-seat Alexander-bodied Leyland Tiger Cub, new in 1964, seen in the coach park opposite Westminster Abbey.

At Waterloo
Road coach park
on 4 August 1966,
WLJ956 is an Albion
Aberdonian with
Harrington Wayfarer
41-seat coachwork,
new to Charlie's Cars
of Bournemouth in
1959, and transferred
to the associated
Shamrock & Rambler
fleet in 1964. In
turn, that fleet has
recently become part
of the nationalised
Transport Holding
Company.

Seen amid a group
of other East Kent
coaches on 5 August
1966, East Kent 1957
Beadle-bodied AEC
Reliance touring
coach MJG50 is
about to disembark
its passengers in
the street outside
Victoria Coach
Station, where there
is no space for it to
do so.

I was back in the North West on Saturday, 6 August 1966, visiting, amongst other places, Stockport. Here at Mersey Square bus station is the North Western Road Car Company's 1949 all-Leyland Titan PD2/1 lowbridge 53-seater No.238. The similar No.250 on the left seats 58.

Stockport Corporation had a batch of all-Leyland Titans too, carrying a similar red and cream livery to that of North Western. No.282 and No.274 are PD2/1s dating from 1948, but have highbridge 56-seat bodywork. They are seen in Heaton Land depot.

On this occasion, I spent the weekend in the North West, travelling across to Liverpool on Sunday, 7 August 1966. At the Corporation's Prince Albert Square depot, the body on this Weymann-framed AEC Regent III, A735 dating from 1950, was completed by Davidson's, one of many local firms contracted to do so. At the period these buses were built, Liverpool suffered a chronic vehicle shortage following the rigours of the Second World War, so it was 'all hands on deck' to provide new vehicles.

A newer Liverpool City Transport AEC Regent III is A21, built in 1953 with Crossley 56-seat bodywork. It is seen at Edge Lane depot.

Crosville was one of two major inter-urban operators serving Liverpool, along with Ribble. At their depot in the city, DKB644 and DKB658 are two of the last Bristol KSWs in their fleet. With standard ECW 55-seat lowbridge bodies, they date from 1953.

An OTC trip to operators in Derbyshire and South Yorkshire on 14 August 1966 took me to Chesterfield, where this very unusual vehicle is seen. JHA836 is a Midland Red S8 single-decker with MCCW 44-seat bodywork new in 1948, now with independent Hulley of Baslow. Very few of Midland Red's 'home made' buses saw use with other operators after withdrawal, but Hulley's had a number of them.

A more conventional Hulley vehicle is DHE350, a 1951 Leyland Royal Tiger with Brush 43-seat bodywork acquired from Yorkshire Traction. Founded in 1921, this Peak District independent bus operator is still going strong today!

Another independent fleet we visited that day was Booth & Fisher of Halfway, near Sheffield. KGY270 is a 1949 Bedford OB with Mulliner 30-seat bodywork, which had been new as a school bus to my original employer, the London County Council! It is now withdrawn in the yard of Booth & Fisher's depot.

Inside the depot, MNU83 is another Bedford OB, one of six supplied new to Booth & Fisher in 1948 with very rare Allsop 29-seat bodies.

Another rare body make to be seen on a Booth & Fisher Bedford OB is that by Barnaby. LRB750 has this make, seating 29, and dates from 1948. It is flanked by two ex-Eastern National ECW-bodied Bristol SC4LK 35-seaters, 9575F and 612JPU, built in 1957 and 1958 respectively.

Yet another Bedford OB with unusual bodywork in Booth & Fisher's fleet is HUO680, which is a Beadle-bodied 29-seater that was new to Western National in 1948.

Another elderly single-decker to be seen on our visit to South Yorkshire on 14 August 1966 is Rotherham Corporation No.117, a Bristol L5G with East Lancs 32-seat centre-entrance bodywork, new in 1950. Up to this time, this operator had standardised on Bristols, but had to look elsewhere for its bus chassis following Bristol's being nationalised and only able to supply them to nationalised fleets – the Tilling Group, London Transport and the Scottish Bus Group.

The main inter-urban operator in this area was Mexborough & Swinton Traction Co. Ltd. This was a BET fleet, who for some reason often acquired surplus vehicles from fellow BET operator Southdown. One such is their No.21, a 1951 all-Leyland Titan PD2/12 58-seater that had been Southdown No.704. It is seen at their Rawmarsh depot in the company of two other ex-Southdown Titans.

Also at Rawmarsh, No.56 is a Leyland Tiger Cub with Weymann 42-seat bodywork, new in 1960.

My summer holiday in 1966 was in Hastings. Unique to the town were three Beadle-bodied AEC Regal Is new in 1946, that had been cut down by owner Maidstone & District in 1956 for use on tours around the town. One of them, OR2, is seen on the seafront on 20 August 1966. The tour cost the princely sum of 1/6d (approx 8p in today's money).

A more conventional Maidstone & District coach is C286, seen at their Hastings depot on 21 August 1966. It is one of the last two all-Leyland Royal Tiger 41-seaters in the fleet, and was new in 1951.

Also at the depot is C351, one of three Harrington-bodied Commer T48B integral 41-seat coaches new in 1956.

Maidstone & District had a batch of Harrington-bodied Commer T48B integral single-deck buses, too, which seated 42. New in 1957, S207 now awaits disposal.

Staying in Hastings enabled me to visit various other towns along the south coast, one being Brighton. Here on 22 August 1966, Southdown 1948 all-Leyland Titan PD2/1 54-seater JCD84 is seen in their Freshfield Road garage. Curiously, it has been retained for relief duties despite being three years older than the Titan sold to Mexborough & Swinton seen earlier.

At Brighton's Pool Valley bus station the same day is Southdown No.523, a Guy Arab IV with Park Royal 57-seat bodywork new in 1955.

Also at Pool Valley, Leyland Titan PD2/12 OCD771 also dates from 1955 and has very similar Park Royal bodywork to the Guy Arab.

Representing Southdown single-deckers of the early 1960s is No.662, a Leyland Tiger Cub with Marshall 43-seat bodywork, new in 1960, and also seen at Pool Valley.

An earlier single-decker seen at the same spot is No.1509, a Royal Tiger with East Lancs bodywork seating 41, new in 1952.

Around the corner at Old Steine, Brighton Corporation No.88 is a 58-seat AEC Regent III with Weymann bodywork, new in 1947, seen working circular service 41. These buses are now due for early withdrawal.

A later Brighton Corporation Regent III also seen at Old Steine on route 41 is No.94, new in 1950 also with Weymann bodywork but seating 56.

On 24 August 1966, I travelled along the coast to Eastbourne, where the Corporation's 1948 East Lancs/Bruce-bodied 56-seat Leyland Titan PD2/1 No.26 is seen at the terminus of their route 2. This Titan is due for early withdrawal.

Seen outside Southdown's Worthing depot on 25 August 1966, No.379 is another 1948 all-Leyland Titan 54-seater retained for relief duties.

Inside Worthing depot, another 1948 Titan PD2/1, No.385, contrasts with 1955 Park Royal-bodied Guy Arab IV 57-seater No.528.

A visitor to the depot is Timpson of Catford's 1957 41-seat Beadle bodied Commer TS3 integral coach TGJ489. Behind it stands one of Southdown's famous 'Queen Mary' Leyland Titan PD3 double-deckers with full-fronted Northern Counties bodywork.

Further along the coast, at Chichester bus station is Southdown 1953 Duple Midland-bodied 39-seat Leyland Tiger Cub No.633.

Another look at Brighton Corporation 1947 Weymann-bodied AEC Regent III No.88, this time at Old Steine on route 53 on 26 August 1966.

Rare survivors by now are a batch of Dennis Lancet J10s with Strachans 38-seat bodywork, new in 1950 to Aldershot & District. Smartly kept No.177 stands in their Guildford depot on 26 August 1966. I managed to reach this point from Hastings by catching a train from Hastings to Sevenoaks and then buying a London Transport 'Green Rover' ticket to travel all the way via Croydon on routes 403 and 408, then back again via Dorking, Reigate, Godstone and Westerham.

A typical scene at seaside resorts in the 1960s was that of coaches offering excursion trips along the seafront. On 28 August 1966, this little Bedford OB, a 27-seater with unusual Plaxton coachwork, advertises tours for its owner, Phillips' Empress Coaches of Hastings, to whom it was new. Behind is a Harrington Wayfarer-bodied AEC Reliance of the town's major operator, Maidstone & District, with whom it is competing.

Now converted to a caravan, OWE18 is a Roe-bodied AEC Regent III new only in 1952 to Sheffield Corporation and originally seating 58. It too is at Hastings on 28 August 1966.

At Hastings' seafront coach park the same day, 1954 Burlingham Seagull-bodied Leyland Tiger Cub 41-seater FDB575 has recently been acquired by Suffolk independent operator Norfolk's of Nayland from Trent Motor Traction. It has a number of London Transport Routemasters on coastal outings for company, with RM1405 from Peckham, Rye Lane garage nearest the camera.

On 29 August 1966, 1956 Harrington-Commer T48B integral 41-seat coach C352, which has Contender coachwork, stands outside Maidstone & District's Hastings depot.

Sadly, the last time I visited the East Kent fleet before it was subsumed into the National Bus Company was on 30 August 1966. Their 1951 Park Royal-bodied Guy Arab III 56-seater FFN367 is seen at Folkestone bus station. The similarity of its bodywork to that of London Transport's RT-types is obvious.

Caught in a heavy rain shower on the same occasion is East Kent YJG808, one of a batch of three 72-seat Park Royal-bodied AEC Bridgemasters, new in 1962 and based at Dover. Though similar in appearance to the much more numerous Regent Vs in the fleet, they look somewhat ungainly. This one saw service with Osborne of Tollesbury, Essex, after withdrawal by East Kent, and was later preserved.

Another trip to Liverpool on 4 September 1966 took me to their Green Lane depot, where the Corporation's A713 (JKF956), a Weymann-bodied AEC Regent III 56-seater new in 1950, is one of several elderly double-deckers awaiting disposal.

Across the road in Gilmoss depot is L39, a Weymann-bodied Leyland Titan PD2/12 new in 1953.

Also at Gilmoss, L479 is a Leyland Titan PD2/1 with Roberts 56-seat bodywork. New in 1951, these buses are now being withdrawn.

At the Earls Court Commercial Motor Show on 24 September 1966, YTB771D is a dual-entrance Leyland Panther Cub with Strachans bodywork and is a demonstrator belonging to Leyland Motors. It exhorts the benefits of such new rear-engined single-deckers, which at the time were all the rage.

Also at Earls Court is Edinburgh Corporation No.801, a Leyland Atlantean with Alexander 'panoramic' bodywork. In later years, the large windows on such buses were prone to leakage of rainwater.

The new Duple Viceroy body was unveiled at the 1966 Commercial Motor show, in this case on an as-yet unregistered Ford R192 chassis destined for Golden Miller Coaches of Feltham.

A visit to Wolverhampton Corporation on 25 September 1966 finds 1948 Brush-bodied Daimler CVD6 No.506 and 1950 Park Royal-bodied Guy Arab III No.552 at their Bilston Street depot. Both are 54-seaters and are due for early withdrawal.

Fishwick of Leyland is a well-known Lancashire independent bus and coach operator, still going strong today. Naturally, they favoured Leyland products, of which their No.8 is an Olympian with 44-seat MCW bodywork, seen in Preston on 8 October 1966. Fishwick had a number of these vehicles, which were quite scarce in the UK, most having been built for the export and colonial market.

Seen on 15 October 1966 in Montague Street, behind the British Museum in Bloomsbury, Wallace Arnold 69BUA is one of the first 36ft-long coaches built for the British market, dating from 1962. It is one of thirteen Leyland Leopards supplied that year with an elongated version of the Plaxton 'Embassy' body, with a centre entrance and seating 49.

An OTC trip visiting Red Rover of Aylesbury on 16 October 1966 finds ex-London Transport RT1668 (KXW314) at their depot. In common with many early RTs sold to other fleets it has had its roof route number box removed. This had been withdrawn at the end of 1962, but was not placed in service with Red Rover until almost two years later, having spent all of 1963 in store in LT garages and most of 1964 with dealer Bird's of Stratford-Upon-Avon. It remained with Red Rover until September 1968.

Red Rover also bought new AECs, of which 27WKX is a very rare Bridgemaster with Park Royal 73-seat rear-entrance bodywork, new in 1958.

Another early ex-London Transport RT, RT211 (HLW198) which has retained its roofbox, is seen with Elms Coaches of Kenton at their depot on 29 October 1966. It had been acquired by them in August 1963 and was withdrawn in June 1970 following a low bridge accident.

On the same day, two British European Airways AEC Regal IVs are seen at Heathrow Airport. MLL810 is a former Green Line coach with MCCW 39-seat coachwork, originally RF273 in the London Transport fleet, and now used as an 'airside coach' ferrying passengers from the airport terminals to the actual aeroplanes. MLL718 is one of 65 Park Royal-bodied 'half deck' coaches (with the rear part of their lower decks used to accommodate luggage) operated and maintained by London Transport for BEA's express coach service between the West London Air Terminal in Earls Court and the airport. These were due for imminent replacement by new Routemaster coaches.

BEA had several other airside coaches which had been acquired from other sources. UYL708 is a Mulliner-bodied Bedford SB3 42-seater, new in 1958 and acquired from the Ministry of Supply in 1965.

BET operator Aldershot & District standardised on Dennises for their double-deck fleet for many years. At Aldershot bus station on 30 October 1966, their No.413 is a Loline III with Alexander 68-seat forward entrance bodywork, new in 1961.

Following the cessation of single-deck chassis building by Dennis, Aldershot & District turned to AEC for their single-deck bus and coach needs. No.329 is a 1958 Weymann-bodied Reliance 41-seater, seen at Guildford.

Seen in Waterloo Road coach park on 21 November 1966, DDE950D is a brand new 45-seat Plaxton-bodied Leyland Leopard PSU4 owned by Silcox of Pembroke Dock.

On a gloomy 3 December 1966, Crosville SLG156 is one of several elderly Bristol L-types still in service at Crewe, being an LL5G with ECW 39-seat rear entrance bodywork, new in 1950.

The following week I was in the north-west again, this time in Manchester, on 10 December 1966. The City Corporation's No.3511 is a 1958 Leyland Titan PD2/40 with Burlingham 65-seat bodywork, seen at Lower Mosley Street bus station. The gentleman standing in front of it is religiously noting its Leyland chassis frame number, which was stamped on the nearside front dumbiron, which usually had to be scraped to reveal its number.

My trip to Manchester was to ride on a farewell tour on their Crossley double-deckers, organised by the PSV Circle. This included a visit to the Corporation's Hyde Road depot disposal yard. Several of them were withdrawn there, including No. 2049, a Crossley-bodied DD42/4 with typical Manchester 58-seat bodywork. Note also the withdrawn trolleybus behind it.

Also withdrawn at Hyde Road is No.4046, a Daimler CVG5 new in 1949 with identical Crossley bodywork.

No.3083 (GVR285) is another doomed Manchester double-decker at Hyde Road. It is one of 200 Leyland Titan PD1s with MCCW 58-seat bodywork, new in 1946–1948, and has lost its engine and been vandalised.

Seen at Waterloo on 7 January 1967, CCW708 typifies the type of unusual coach that could be seen in use as workmen's buses by building contractors at this period. It is an Atkinson Alpha PM746H with extremely rare Trans-United 41-seat centre-entrance coachwork new to Bracewell's Coaches of Colne in 1954, now with Stanley Hugh Leach of Yeading.

On the same day, OVD857, a Plaxton-bodied Albion MR11L 41-seater, new to Hutchinson of Overtown in 1957, is seen in Midland Road, St. Pancras, operated by Croot's Coaches of Sandy, Beds.

At Grey Green's Stamford Hill headquarters and coach station on 11 February 1967, 852FXP is a 1963 Duple Bella Vega-bodied Bedford SB, in the livery of their subsidiary Viney's Coaches. Following Grey Green's metamorphosis into a London bus operator in the 1980s and their subsequent takeover by Arriva, these premises were closed and demolished. Reizel Close, an exclusive development for Stamford Hill's ultra-orthodox Jewish community, now occupies the site.

Super Coaches of Upminster was another well-known independent operator in the London area, forerunner of today's Ensignbus. They had a number of former London Transport buses, which at this time were often hired back to LT for special services their own staff would not work owing to an overtime ban. On 18 February 1967, lowbridge Weymann-bodied AEC Regent III KYY503, former RLH3 in the LT fleet, is an odd choice for the football express service from Manor House tube station to Tottenham Hotspur's ground. Note its smartly turned-out clippie on the right.

Next day, 19 February 1967, I was up in the Midlands again for the first time in 1967. Here at Mansfield bus station is Trent No.495, a brand new Alexander-bodied Daimler Fleetline upon which I had ridden there from Nottingham.

Mansfield District Bristol FSF6G 60-seat Lodekka No.542, one of ten delivered to the company in 1961/62, is also seen in Mansfield bus station. Not many FSs with forward entrances like this were delivered; the majority had rear entrances.

Seen at Bressenden Place, Victoria, on 25 February 1967, NWC699 is a Bedford SB5 with Burlingham Gannet 41-seat bodywork new to Southcott of Loughton in 1962, now operated by Evan Evans Tours, a well-known London coach company specialising in luxury tours. On this occasion, it has taken theatregoers to the nearby Victoria Palace Theatre.

A well-known independent operator in Wolverhampton was Don Everall. In addition to modern coaches used on touring and private hire work, they also had a number of second-hand double-deckers for school and industrial contracts. One is HG8884, a 1946 Weymann-bodied Leyland Titan PD1 56-seater new to Burnley, Colne & Nelson Joint Transport Committee in 1946. It is seen overtaking a Wolverhampton Corporation trolleybus on their last day of service, 5 March 1967.

Also in Wolverhampton that day is Midland Red No.5246, a 1963 Alexander-bodied Daimler Fleetline, seen beneath the trolleybus wires, bound for Birmingham on route 196 from Stafford. Midland Red was the major inter-urban and rural operator in the West Midlands.

Don Everall was also a vehicle dealer, and this strange vehicle seen in their yard is former London Transport TT4 (527FJJ), one of five Thames Traders with Strachans bodywork built in 1963 to carry cyclists through the new Dartford Tunnel. The centre of the lower deck housed cycle racks, whilst the cyclists rode on the upper deck, which was accessed by a rather steep stairway on both sides of the vehicle. Few people used the service, which was withdrawn after only a few months, rendering these special buses surplus. For some reason, this one survived and today has been preserved by Ensignbus at Purfleet, not far from the Dartford Tunnel.

One of several real oddities at Wembley on 11 March 1967 is Norfolk's of Nayland's early AEC Regal IV LWT147, carrying a very rare centre-entrance Whitson coach body. It was new in May 1952 to Yorkshire independent operator Ripponden & District, and contrasts with two more recent Duple-bodied Bedfords parked behind it, at least one of which is a VAL.

On 12 March 1967, brand new Aldershot & District MCW-bodied AEC Reliance 41-seater No.542 departs from Winchester bus station for Aldershot. This was one of the last 30ft-long AEC Reliances to be built.

Another new single-decker in Winchester that day is King Alfred's GHO416D, a 1966 Strachans-bodied Bedford VAM5, seen loading up in the city centre bound for Basingstoke. Nowadays, this operator's routes are re-created here with preserved buses each New Year's Day.

This scene at Maidstone's Lower Stone Street bus station on 15 March 1967 sees two of Maidstone & District's 1951 all-Leyland Titan PD2 56-seaters, DH385 and DH402, along with a wartime Bristol K rebodied by Weymann and a later Titan PD2 with similar bodywork.

Seen on 18 March 1967, FJA680 is an elderly Dennis Lancet J3 with full-fronted Plaxton coachwork apparently dumped on wasteground in Hounslow. It had latterly been with Brocklehurst Coaches.

The first OTC trip of 1967 took us to various operators in Warwickshire on 19 March 1967. The first was Priory Coaches of Leamington, who had a number of ex-Coventry Corporation double-deckers. One is EKV821, a 1943 Daimler CWG5 still with original Massey wartime utility bodywork, seen at their depot.

Another independent operator nearby was G&G Coaches of Leamington. Their SHA455 is a former Midland Red all-Leyland Titan PD2/12 56-seater new in 1955 as their No.4055, one of 100 such buses classified by them as class LD8.

A Leyland Titan PD2 of a different origin seen in G&G's depot is LUC71, former London Transport RTL1147. Has the young bus spotter emerging from the shadows on the left 'copped' it, or had he seen it in London already?

Priory Coaches had a number of Leyland Titan PD2s, too, one of which is all-Leyland JUE359 which had been new to Stratford-Upon-Avon Blue Motor Services in 1950.

Next on our agenda that day was Coventry Corporation, at whose Harnall Lane East depot No.166 is a Daimler CVG6 with MCW 60-seat bodywork. It is the first of the batch of 125 built between 1955 and 1959. It accompanies No.50, a Daimler CVA6 with Birmingham-style MCCW bodywork dating from 1949 and now demoted to training duties.

Typical of former major company vehicles employed as workmen's transport at this period is EFV626, a former Ribble all-Leyland Royal Tiger coach now with the major contractor Wimpey. It passes London's Aldgate station on 22 March 1967.

South Midland was the coaching arm of Tilling Group company Thames Valley, working express services to such places as Oxford. On Easter Saturday, 25 March 1967, their No.85 is seen at Victoria Coach Station. Things are not what they seem, however, since despite its standard ECW 39-seat coachwork, it is an AEC Regal IV and not a Bristol LS as would be expected.

A more exotic visitor to Victoria Coach Station that day is Highland Omnibuses' GSS804, a Duple Firefly-bodied Thames Trader touring coach, which has worked down to London on hire to Eastern Scottish. It arouses the interest of one of the coach station's inspectors, seen on the right.

Seen in a rather wet Newport bus station on 8 April 1967, 98EAX is No.110 in the fleet of Jones of Aberbeeg. It is a Willowbrook-bodied AEC Reliance 45-seater, new in 1962.

Seen at Wembley for the Amateur Cup Final on 22 April 1967 is 7672EV, a 1959 Thurgood-bodied Bedford SB3 41-seater belonging to Leicestershire independent coach operator Charnwood Coaches. It had been new to Ward's Coaches of Epping.

Also at Wembley that day is BTD871E, a brand new MCW Metropolitan-bodied Bedford VAM5 belonging to Walls of Wigan.

Also from Wigan, 2049LG is not what it seems. It is an early 1950s Leyland Royal Tiger PSU1/11, originally registered LRH56, whose chassis was lengthened to 36ft and given a new Plaxton Panorama 51-seat body in April 1963.

Another early Royal Tiger, of type PSU1/15, is GBU834 with Crown Coaches of Liverpool. This one, however, is still of its original length, and was given a new Plaxton Panorama 41-seat body in August 1965.

477AJJ is a Burlingham Seagull 70-bodied Thames Trader 570E 41-seater new in 1960, operated by W. A. Baldwin's Coaches of Lower Edmonton. The supporters it brought to the match must have been frustrated, since the result was Enfield 0, Skelmersdale 0. However, at a replay at Manchester City's ground a week later, the London team won 3-0.

Next day, I was on an OTC trip to the famous Hampshire independent operator Gosport & Fareham (Provincial) on 23 April 1967. At their Hoeford depot, CG9606 is a 1934 AEC Regal with full-fronted Reading 34-seat bodywork, new in 1958. This operator was renowned for keeping such elderly vehicles in service, and sister bus CG9607 is preserved today.

A more mundane Provincial vehicle is their No.62 (FCR198), a Park Royal-bodied Guy Arab III 56-seater that had been new to Southampton Corporation in 1948.

We also visited Southampton Corporation that day, where their virtually identical 1951 Guy Arab III No.242 is seen in their Shirley depot. The Corporation standardised on this type of double-decker in the early post-war years.

Our next port of call was Hants & Dorset's Southampton depot, in which are seen their 1952 Bristol LL6B/ECW 37-seater No.786 and open topper No.1137. This is a 1948 Bristol K5G with a 1945 Strachan 59-seat body which had been removed from an earlier vehicle and converted to open-top.

Back at Wembley on 29 April 1967, this time for the schoolboys' international football final played between England and Scotland, Reliance of Newbury 1955 Burlingham Seagull-bodied AEC Reliance 41-seater No.36 (LBL197) arrives alongside a newer Reliance belonging to Maidstone & District.

Leading a group of more modern coaches, elderly Duple Vista-bodied Bedford OB 29-seater MME738 belongs to a scout group. By now, such specimens were becoming rare.

One of many ex-major company double-deckers at Wembley that day is GNJ998, a 60-seat ECW-bodied Bristol KSW6B that had been new to Brighton, Hove & District as their No.6431 in May 1952. It is now in the fleet of Super Coaches of Upminster, and usually used for school contracts.

Another elderly Duple Vista-bodied Bedford OB seen at Wembley is HCG947, owned by Reg's Coaches of Welwyn Garden City, Herts.

Another ex-Tilling Group ECW-bodied Bristol at Wembley is GHR366, owned by my local operator, Cornwallis Coaches of Holloway. It is a K5G with 55-seat lowbridge bodywork, originally new in 1950 as No.302 in the Wilts & Dorset fleet.

Due for early withdrawal at this time are Reading Corporation's 1950 Crossley DD42/8s No.86 and No.87, with lowbridge 52-seat Crossley bodywork. Twelve of these were built for the Corporation and by now were only used during rush hours when seen at their Mill Lane depot on 30 April 1967.

A visit to Brighton on 7 May 1967 finds LUV353, a 1950 Dennis Lancet J3 new to Glenton Tours and given a new full-front Plaxton 30-seat body in March 1957. It is devoid of any ownership details, so is presumably now a non-PSV.

Also now a non-PSV, former Maidstone & District wartime Bristol K6A DH159 (HKE867) which was rebodied by Weymann in 1951 is accompanied by Plaxton and Duple-bodied coaches, the latter being a new Bedford with Ronsway of Hemel Hempstead.

Seen arriving at Wembley on 13 May 1967, Smith's Tours of Wigan CEK588D is a very odd vehicle indeed. It is one of two coaches owned by this company based on Leyland Olympic chassis that had been on board a ship bound for Cuba which sank in the Thames Estuary in 1964. They were retrieved and given Van Hool 44-seat centre entrance bodies in 1966, being some of the first post-war British coaches to be bodied in Continental Europe. They also retained left-hand drive, as clearly seen here, for touring in Europe.

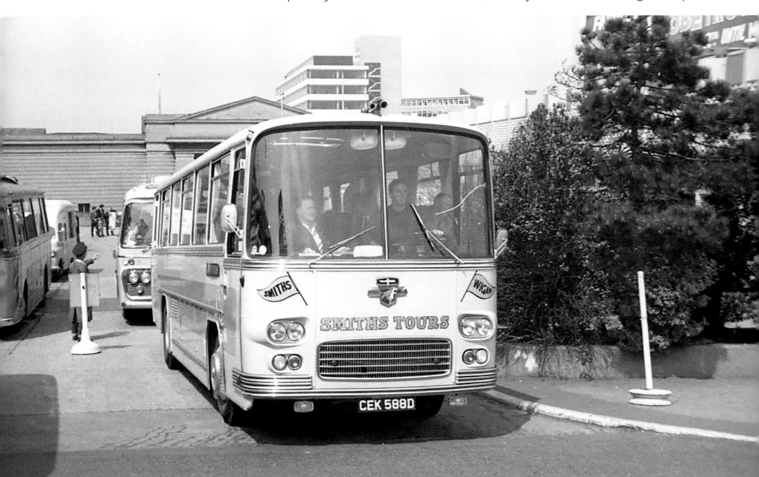

Also very unusual, 504WLG of Sportsman Coaches of Whiston is an early 1950s Leyland Royal Tiger PSU1/15 whose chassis has been lengthened to accommodate a 36-foot long Plaxton Panorama body, fitted in August 1962. It is also seen at Wembley.

By 20 May 1967, early ECW-bodied Bristol LS coaches were being withdrawn by Tilling Group operators and therefore becoming available on the second-hand market to small independent fleets. An example of this is 1953 LS6G 41-seater LTA997, formerly Southern National No.1341 and now a non-PSV with Martin of Weaverham. It is seen parked in Bloomsbury.

A visit to Sheffield on 21 May 1967 finds the City Corporation's No.696, a 1954 Leyland Titan PD2/12 with 58-seat MCCW bodywork working route 14. This was a typical vehicle in their fleet, composed mainly of AEC and Leyland vehicles at the time.

The following Sunday, 28 May 1967, I was in Liverpool visiting British Railways' steam motive power depots, but also found time to look at the City Corporation's buses, too. In their Garston depot are two AEC Regent IIIs, A35 with Crossley 'tin-front' 56-seat bodywork new in 1953, and A769, new in 1951 also with Crossley 56-bodywork, but having a traditional exposed radiator. This large fleet was composed mainly of AEC and Leyland vehicles.

As in London with the sole RM664, Liverpool Corporation tried 'unpainted' aluminium buses. One is 1957 Leyland PD2/20 L306, with Crossley/LCPT bodywork seating 62.

An OTC visit on 11 June 1967 to Barton's Chilwell headquarters witnessed many interesting vehicles in that operator's varied fleet. Their No.855 is a 1947 all-Leyland Titan PD1 lowbridge 53-seater, acquired from Western Welsh in 1960.

In contrast, Barton No.1027 is a Bedford SB5 with Yeates 43-seat coachwork acquired from Price of Halesowen in 1965. It was new in 1962.

An older coach in Barton's fleet is No.725, one of their famous BTS rebuilds using parts from pre-war Leyland Lions, new in 1954 with a Plaxton 37-seat body.

No.790 in Barton's fleet is also a rebuild, but of a post-war Leyland Tiger PS1, originally a single-decker, given this Northern Counties 61-seat double-deck body in 1957. There were a number of similar rebuilds in the fleet.

We also visited Mansfield District that day. Outside their Sutton Road depot in Mansfield, prototype ECW-bodied Bristol VRSL6G 78-seater HHW933D, a Bristol Commercial Vehicles demonstrator on loan to the company, has just changed crew. Vehicles of this type were now being made available to non-Tilling Group fleets. This one, however, became C5001 in Bristol Omnibuses' fleet in May 1970.

Another enthusiasts' visit on 18 June 1967 took me to Staffordshire independent operator Harper Brothers of Heath Hayes. One of a number of elderly half-cab coaches still in use with them is their No.44 (TRE824), a Leyland Tiger PS2/3 with Burlingham 33-seat bodywork, new to the company in May 1950.

With attractive Duple Northern Alpine Continental 51-seat bodywork, 4779NE is a Leyland Leopard PSU3/3R, new to Happiways of Manchester in July 1963. It is seen in Hanley on 18 June 1967.

We visited Potteries Motor Traction's Hanley depot on the same occasion. Their S678 is a 1956 AEC Reliance with Burlingham 44-seat bodywork, one of two acquired with the business of Baxter of Hanley in 1958. Potteries acquired several small independent fleets in its area during this period, giving rise to a varied fleet.

Potteries H7700 is a one-off Leyland Titan PD3/2 new in 1956 with Metro-Cammell Orion 30ft-long 68-seat bodywork, produced at a time when double-deckers of this length had just been authorised. It is seen at their Stoke-On-Trent depot.

Inside the depot, C7716 is one of five Commer T48B-Beadle 41-seat integral coaches new to Potteries in 1957.

A brand new coach to be found in London's Waterloo Road coach park next day, 19 June 1967, is Alexander Midland Duple Viceroy-bodied Bedford VAM coach MW278, which has brought a party down from Scotland.

Back in Potteries' area the following Saturday, 24 June 1967, PRF759 is an elderly Leyland Tiger PS1 with unusual Lawton coachwork in use as a towing vehicle at their Longton depot. It was acquired with the business of Stanier, Newchapel in 1965 and adapted for this role.

A well-known independent operator in this area was Beresford of Cheddleton, who were renowned for collecting elderly second-hand vehicles, which had either been withdrawn by them or merely acquired for spare parts, at their depot. Their No.32 is a 1950 Daimler CVG6 with Metro-Cammell 54-seat bodywork acquired from Salford City Transport which is still in use; the other Daimler in the picture, DBR43, is a 1953 Roe-bodied CVG5 acquired from Sunderland Corporation for spares only.

The only municipal operator within London Transport's operating area was Luton Corporation, whose buses sported a red and cream livery similar to LT's Central Area buses, though of course it was their Country Area green buses that served the town. On 25 June 1967, their No.119, now one of the oldest buses in the fleet, stands in the rain outside their depot. It is one of twelve all-Leyland Titan PD2/1s with 53-seat lowbridge bodywork, new in 1948.

On the same day, United Counties 1952 ECW-bodied Bristol KSW5G lowbridge 55-seater No.882 stands outside their Biggleswade depot. This was one of many vehicles acquired from Eastern National when that company's operations in Bedfordshire, Buckinghamshire, North Hertfordshire and Huntingdonshire were transferred to them in May 1952.

On 1 July 1967, I was back in the North West again, this time on the Wirral peninsula, for both BR steam and for the local bus operators. This view shows Birkenhead Corporation No.193, a 1950 Guy Arab III with Massey 56-seat bodywork, now relegated to driver training duties. It is seen in their Laird Street depot.

Birkenhead favoured Massey bodies for many years. No.358 is another example, seating 59 and mounted on a Guy Arab IV chassis. It was new in 1955 and is seen in the town centre.

A smaller municipal operator on the Wirral was Wallasey Corporation. Despite its virtually pre-war appearance, their No.39 is a Leyland Titan PD2/1 with Metro-Cammell 56-seat bodywork, new in 1950. It is seen in their Liscard depot.

Back in Birkenhead, that Corporation's No.144 is a brand new Leyland Titan PD3, again with Massey bodywork, seen at New Ferry terminus. Both Birkenhead and Wallasey Corporations would be subsumed within the Merseyside PTE in 1969.

Crosville was the major inter-urban operator in this area. One of the oldest buses in their fleet at this time is DKA172, a 1944 Bristol K5G originally with wartime utility bodywork, but given this new ECW 55-seat lowbridge body in 1953. It is seen on local route F19 from Heswall, also at New Ferry terminus.

A visit to Matlock on 2 July 1967 finds North Western 1953 Weymann-bodied Leyland Royal Tiger PSU1/13 44-seater No.543 in the town's bus station.

A very smart vehicle to be seen in Wakefield on 8 July 1967 is Duple-bodied Daimler CVD6 lowbridge 56-seater LTO10, which had been new to Skills of Nottingham in 1950, in the fleet of W. R. Bingley, one of three small independent operators who ran a service from here to Doncaster under the name of United Services.

A better-known and much larger independent fleet based in Wakefield was West Riding, whose 1955 Roe-bodied Guy Arab IV 53-seater is one of two seen in the town's bus station.

An older West Riding vehicle, seen arriving in Leeds city centre the same day, is No.633, an all-Leyland lowbridge Titan PD2/1 53-seater new in 1948.

Leeds City Transport also had a number of Leyland PD2 Titans. No.302, seen in the city centre, is one of ten PD2/14s with Roe 58-seat bodywork, supplied in 1953.

Leeds' fleet had many more AEC Regents than they had Leyland Titans. Two of them are seen in the city's central bus station – No.888 is a 1957 Regent V with Roe 60-seat bodywork, unusually with an exposed radiator, whilst No.700 is a solitary Regent III built in 1950 with an 8ft-wide Roe 56-seat body. This vehicle's extra width is quite apparent when compared to No.888, which is 7ft 6ins wide.

Another smart Leeds City AEC Regent III is No.653, which has Weymann 58-seat bodywork and was new in 1953. Here it is arriving at the central bus station.

Also in the bus station is 6237UB, a 1960 Leyland Titan PD3/1 with Roe 73-seat bodywork, in the fleet of Wallace Arnold's subsidiary Kippax Motors.

Another independent fleet serving Leeds was that of Samuel Ledgard. More than 30 ex-London Transport RTs were in their fleet at this time, but only a couple of RTLs. One was KYY799, formerly RTL829, which had been acquired in October 1966. One of the Metro-Cammell-bodied batch, it saw two years' more service in Scotland after the Ledgard business ceased.

Major operators West Yorkshire, Yorkshire Traction and Yorkshire Woollen District all served Leeds, too. No.699 in the latter fleet is a 1951 Leyland Tiger PS2, which was originally a single-decker, but given a new Roe 63-seat forward-entrance double-deck body in 1963.

On 15 July 1967, Scottish Omnibuses' 1962 AEC Reliance 38-seater B910 typifies modern Alexander-bodied coaches used on overnight services between Scotland and Victoria Coach Station, where it is arriving to collect its passengers after laying over during the day. As so often on summer Saturdays here, pandemonium reigns, with a United Automobile Services Bristol MW coach either loading or unloading in the street on the left.

Another United vehicle does the same, as Southdown 1956 Beadle-bodied Leyland Tiger Cub PSUC1/2 coach No.1055 arrives at the coach station.

A splendid sight to greet me as I left my office at County Hall at lunchtime on 21 July 1967 was three of East Kent's 1957 Beadle-bodied AEC Reliance touring coaches parked outside in Chicheley Street.

Back at Victoria next day, 22 July 1967, Southdown 1957 Commer TS3-Beadle integral coach No.15 arrives at the coach station in less hectic conditions than seen earlier!

An odd sight to be seen in Highbury Hill on 24 August 1967 is JTX667, an AEC Regal III with Burlingham 33-seat coachwork that had been new to Edwards of Beddau in 1950. It is now apparently with a contractor.

An oddity seen at the premises of Green Bus, Rugeley, on 29 July 1967 is URF873, a Foden PVFE6 with King & Taylor full-fronted 38-seat bodywork. It was sold for scrap in April 1968 and only ever had one owner.

Almost as unusual, Green Bus BSD294 is a Daimler CVG6 with Alexander lowbridge 57-seat bodywork that had been new to Western SMT as their No.945 in 1952.

Another independent operator in this area was Stevenson of Spath. They had several ex-London Transport buses, notably former RTW178 (KLB908), seen here in appalling weather at their depot. It remained in service with them until late 1977 and has subsequently been preserved in their distinctive yellow and black livery.

The RTW is accompanied by this non-standard ex-LT Craven-bodied RT1466 (KGK725) which Stevenson's had acquired early in 1957. It ran for them until July 1971, therefore seeing service here twice as long as it did in London.

To accompany ex-LT RTs, RTLs and RTWs, ECW-bodied Guy Special MXX371 had been LT GS71, and was acquired in 1965 after more than two years stored out of use in LT's Garston garage. It too was withdrawn in 1971.

An unusual-looking vehicle with Stevenson's is PRE607, an early post-war Leyland Tiger PS1/1 given a new 8ft-wide Burlingham 35-seat full-fronted coach body in June 1953.

Seen outside Green Bus of Rugeley's offices and waiting room in Burton-On-Trent is their No.18 (JOW918), a Park Royal-bodied Guy Arab UF single-decker that had been new to Southampton Corporation in 1954.

Burton-On-Trent Corporation favoured Guy vehicles, of which their No.4 is seen in their Horninglow Street depot. Despite looking very much like a wartime utility vehicle, it is in fact a 1947 Guy Arab III with Roberts lowbridge 53-seat bodywork.

Another elderly Guy with this Corporation is No.45, also an Arab III dating from 1948 with Guy 35-seat rear entrance single-deck bodywork. It is apparently undergoing attention to its engine outside in the rain.

Yet another Burton Guy is No.11, which has Davies 56-seat bodywork and is an Arab III new in 1950. It has just crossed the River Trent in the pouring rain.

The rain also lashes down on Stevenson's No.15 (KGU69), a Metro-Cammell-bodied RTL recently acquired from London Transport, whose RTL619 it had been until sale in June 1967. Unfortunately, it was to be wrecked in a collision in October 1968 and scrapped as a result.

Midland Red was the major inter-urban operator serving Burton-on-Trent. Their No.4398 is one of 200 of their self-built class D7 double-deckers with Willowbrook 63 seat bodies, new between 1955 and 1957.

Tailby & George Blue Bus was a famous independent operator based in the village of Willington, where their 1951 Willowbrook-bodied Daimler CD650 55-seater just fits beneath a low railway bridge on its way from Derby to Burton-on-Trent.

Burlingham Seagull-bodied coach 120JRB, a rather rare Daimler Freeline new in June 1959, is seen in the Blue Bus Willington depot. Sadly, a disastrous fire at this depot in January 1976 destroyed many of the fleet's interesting vehicles.

The rain is still falling as we arrive in Derby. Their Corporation's No.107 is one of five unusual Foden PVD6s with Brush 56-seat bodywork, new in 1951.

In appalling weather, Derby Corporation tower wagon RC4248 passes British Railways' Derby Locomotive Works. This has been converted from a pre-war Daimler COG double-decker, and its services will no longer be required for Derby's trolleybuses a few weeks later, when they will be withdrawn.

Early on the morning of Sunday, 30 July 1967, Cream Coaches' 1959 Duple Vega-bodied Bedford SB8 41-seat coach WUU552 crosses the junction of Canonbury Lane and Upper Street, Islington, just around the corner from my home in those days, on its way to operate a day trip to Southend.

My OTC trip that day was to South Yorkshire, starting with Doncaster Corporation. At their depot is No.22, an AEC Regal III with Roe 39-seat bodywork built as late as 1953, by which time underfloor-engined single-deckers were rapidly ousting half-cabs.

The rather odd appearance of Doncaster Corporation's 1947 Leyland Titan PD2 No.93 is explained by the fact that it has been rebodied using a Roe body built only in 1958 for a trolleybus!

The same tour took us to various independent stage-carriage operators in Yorkshire. At the depot of H. Wilson's Premier fleet in Stainforth is MWW891, a 1954 Guy Arab IV with Park Royal 61-seat bodywork finished by Guy. On the right of the picture is a preserved Doncaster Corporation trolleybus with similar Roe bodywork to that re-fitted to Leyland Titan buses as seen above.

A very unusual vehicle in the Premier fleet is HBE260, a pre-war AEC Regal (originally registered ABE961) whose chassis was lengthened to 30ft and given a new Saunders 39-seat rear entrance bodywork by the Lincolnshire Road Car Company in June 1951, becoming their No.773. It was acquired by Premier in February 1963.

Another independent operator in the area was R. Store's Reliance of Stainforth. These two elderly vehicles are dumped at their depot; EJW456 is a Guy Arab III new in 1947 with very rare Lawton 37-seat coachwork, similar to the Potteries' towing bus seen earlier, new to Don Everall of Wolverhampton.

In Reliance's operational fleet, 539DWT is a Yeates-bodied SB5 fitted out as a dual-purpose 44-seater, new in March 1963. It is accompanied by two Duple-bodied Bedfords.

7014YG is a very smart Roe-bodied Guy Arab IV forward-entrance 73-seater new to Samuel Morgan's Blue Line of Armthorpe in January 1962.

Yet another independent stage carriage operator in this area was T. Severn & Sons Ltd of Dunscroft. Their KWW514 is a Roe-bodied Leyland Titan PD2/10 56-seater new in 1951, now out of use in their yard.

In Severn & Sons' modern depot, 1956 Park Royal-bodied AEC Reliance 41-seater PYG605 accompanies KWX549, a Leyland Royal Tiger PSU1/15 with Duple Ambassador 41-seat coachwork new in 1951.

Also in T. Severn's depot is EPM13, a standard ECW-bodied Bristol K5G with ECW 56-seat bodywork that had been new as Brighton, Hove & District No.6416 in 1950, and NWY777, a Roe-bodied Leyland Titan PD2/10 57-seater new to them in 1954.

Back in Doncaster that day, Leon of Finningley's 1954 Weymann Orion-bodied AEC Regent III 58-seater PDV731 leaves the bus station. It had been new to Devon General in 1954.

Buses from Rotherham Corporation served the bus station, too – their No.163, an AEC Reliance with Weymann 45-seat bodywork new in 1957, leaves for Sheffield.

Doncaster Corporation's buses also ran to Sheffield – here is their No.37, an unusual Leyland Royal Tiger RTC1/1 with Roe dual-entrance 45-seat bodywork, new in 1965.

Seen leaving Doncaster bus station for Scunthorpe is Lincolnshire 1957 ECW-bodied LD6G Bristol Lodekka 60-seater No.2345.

Seen at the Wilton Road entrance to Victoria station on 4 August 1967, YXH862 is a Duple-bodied Bedford SB8 41-seater with Empress Coaches of Cambridge Heath, another operator still going strong today. It had been new to Advance of Leytonstone in 1960.

An array of Lancashire United's varied fleet is seen in their Swinton depot on 5 August 1967. Nearest the camera is No.518, a 1954 Guy Arab UF with Weymann 40-seat dual-purpose bodywork.

At their Atherton depot and works, No.265 is one of the last Guy Arab Vs built, and has just been delivered. It has Northern Counties 73-seat bodywork.

Inside Atherton depot, No.533 is a Guy Arab IV with Northern Counties 57-seat bodywork, new in 1954. Lancashire United was Britain's largest independent bus and coach operator at this period.

On the same day, Wigan Corporation No.96 is seen in its hometown. It is a typical all-Leyland Titan PD2/12 56-seater, new in 1953.

A newer Wigan vehicle, No.9 is one of three Leyland Titan PD2/30s with Massey 61-seat bodywork, new in 1958. It is seen outside the Corporation's depot.

On 6 August 1967, TOB377 is a Burlingham Seagull-bodied AEC Reliance with the well-known East Anglian independent operator Mulley's Motorways of Ixworth. It is seen at Great Yarmouth.

An OTC trip on this day took me to Great Yarmouth, where seen at their Caister Road depot is the Corporation's No.56, a Leyland Atlantean PDR1/2 with Roe 65-seat bodywork, new in November 1966.

Seen in the town centre, Great Yarmouth No.44 is one of four AEC Regent Vs with Massey 61-seat bodies in the Corporation's fleet, new in 1959.

Great Yarmouth Corporation also had Daimlers in their fleet. No.12 is one of three CVG6s with Roe forward-entrance 61-seat bodies supplied in 1961.

No.82 in Great Yarmouth's fleet is an unusual-looking AEC Reliance with Pennine Coachcraft 39-seat bodywork, one of six delivered in 1964.

No.49 was one of the oldest buses in the Corporation's fleet at this time. It is one of four all-Leyland Titan PD2/10 56-seaters built for them in 1952. Note the advertisement on the wall on the right for the inevitable Morecambe & Wise seaside show.

Also in Great Yarmouth that day is Eastern Counties' coach LS822. This is a Bristol MW6G with the later style of ECW 39-seat coachwork, new in 1963. It is one of several that carry the fleetname of Metropolitan Coaches of Great Yarmouth, which this Tilling Group company had acquired many years previously.

At Eastern Counties' Great Yarmouth depot, LM923 (WVX443) and LM926 (WVX444) are two 1953 ECW-bodied 45-seat Bristol LS5Gs transferred from Tilling Group fleet Eastern National in 1966.

On 9 August 1967, Mulliner bodied Bedford OB 30-seat school bus WVX27 is seen at Turnpike Lane station. Originally belonging to Middlesex County Council, it was inherited by the London Borough of Haringey on 1 April 1965, when that authority was abolished and its schools devolved to the relevant London boroughs.

Scottish operator Western SMT was unusual in having a depot on English soil in Carlisle. Here on 26 August 1967, their No.1628, a very late Bristol LD6G Lodekka with standard ECW 60-seat bodywork, new in 1961, stands outside it.

There were not many single-deckers in the Bolton Corporation fleet, but No.9 was one of two Leyland Royal Tiger PSUI/14s. It has East Lancs 43-seat bodywork and was new in 1955. It is seen outside their depot on 29 August 1967.

In Warrington the same day, 29 August 1967, the Corporation's No.89 is one of two Leyland Titan PD2/40s seen outside the station. Bodywork is East Lancs 65-seat, and they were new in 1962. I was able to visit these operators thanks to a weekly London Midland Region railrover ticket, which took me all the way from my home in Canonbury to Carlisle, where I stayed in order to travel to bus operators and British Railways steam motive power depots alike!

An unusual single-decker in the Sunderland Corporation fleet is No. 47, an Atkinson BPL746HF with Marshall 45-seat dual-entrance bodywork, new in 1964. It is seen in the town centre on 30 August 1967.

With similar Marshall bodywork, Sunderland No.50 is a Leyland Panther Cub, new in 1965.

At the same spot with reconstruction work on Sunderland's town centre progressing in the background, No.267 is a Daimler Fleetline CRG6LX with Roe 77-seat bodywork built in 1964, representing the newer double-deckers in the Corporation's fleet.

A curious vehicle seen at Wallasey Corporation's Liscard depot on 9 September 1967 is No.81. It has a 1957 Leyland Titan PD2/10 chassis usually bodied as a double-decker, but is fitted with a second-hand Burlingham 29-seat coach body, new in 1948.

Consecutively registered No.43 is equally odd. This too has a 1957 PD2/10 chassis, which is fitted with a 1951 Metro-Cammell 56-seat body that had been new to the original No.43, whose chassis had been destroyed in 1959. Where was this chassis between 1957 and 1959?

Seen in Blackpool on 9 September 1967 is Western SMT No.1890, a Leyland Leopard PSU3/3R with Alexander 49-seat coachwork new in 1964.

At Lancashire United's Atherton depot on 10 September 1967, No.646 is one of 14 Leyland Titan PD3/4s with Metro-Cammell 73-seat 30ft-long bodies new in 1958.

A visit to Bradford on 7 October 1967 finds the Corporation's No.18 in the city centre. It is one of 40 Weymann-bodied AEC Regent III 56-seaters new in 1949/50.

Under the trolleybus wires at Bradford's Forster Square is another Weymann-bodied AEC Regent III, MLL838, one of more than 30 ex-London Transport RTs owned by the famous independent operator Samuel Ledgard of Leeds. Sadly, this fleet was taken over by Tilling Group operator West Yorkshire, one of whose Bristol KSWs follows the RT, a few days after this picture was taken, and its interesting vehicles dispersed. This RT, which was originally RT3528 and ended its LT career with a green roofbox body, would return to London for use as a sightseeing bus for a few years.

My last visit to Birmingham City Transport, on an OTC tour on 15 October 1967, finds their 1947 MCCW-bodied Daimler CVG6 54-seater No.1588 out of action, but retained as a snow-clearance vehicle. It has chains on its rear wheels for this work.

Nicely posed outside Birmingham's Rosebery Street garage, No.2214 is one of 50 Leyland Titan PD2s new in 1949/50 with Park Royal 54-seat bodywork.

A wet day at Bell Corner, Walthamstow, 22 February 1968, sees by pure coincidence two elderly vehicles that originated in the Bristol area. SAE952 is a Duple-bodied Bedford SBO coach new to Wessex Motorways in 1954, whilst LHY545 is a former Bristol Omnibus Company ECW-bodied Bristol K, new in 1950. The latter is one of several in use for school transport with the London Borough of Waltham Forest.

Seen at Wembley on 2 March 1968, OTS603 is an oddity in the fleet of Wallace Arnold of Leeds. It is a Bedford VAL14 with Plaxton Panorama 49-seat coachwork, new to Dickson of Dundee in 1963, whose business was acquired by Wallace Arnold the same year.

Another Plaxton-bodied vehicle at Wembley that day is 79BLT, an AEC Reliance new to Glenton Tours and now with North London firm Finchley Coaches. A former London Transport RT and Leicester City Transport Leyland Titan PD2 follow.

With another London operator, Duple Northern Continental-bodied AEC Reliance 540DYO has recently been acquired by Valliant Cronshaw from Global Tours, London W1, to whom it was new in June 1962 as one of the earliest examples of this style of coach body built.

The following week at Wembley, 9 March 1968, Southdown Beadle-Commer integral coach No.6 arrives neck-and-neck with Dawson's Coaches' Plaxton Panorama-bodied Bedford VAL14 1543DH.

Arriving at Wembley the same day, 510ERO is an AEC Reliance with Roe Dalesman 41-seat coachwork, new to Brunt's Coaches of Bell Bar, Herts, in 1959.

Another AEC Reliance at Wembley that day is FUP272C, which has Willowbrook 49-seat dual-purpose bodywork and was new to Weardale of Frosterly in February 1965. Now with Stanhope Motor Services Ltd, it was later acquired by Barton of Chilwell.

The first OTC trip of the 1968 season visited various operators in East Anglia on 17 March 1968. One was Eastern Counties, whose 1949 ECW-bodied Bristol K5G 56-seater LKH427 is now one of the oldest buses in the fleet. It is seen here at Norwich bus station.

Another elderly vehicle seen there is LL740, a 39-seat rear-entrance ECW-bodied Bristol LWL5G, new in 1951.

We also visited Lowestoft that day. With similar ECW bodywork to that of the Eastern Counties Bristol K5G seen earlier, the Corporation's No.27 is one of nine AEC Regent II 56-seaters built in 1947, still going strong 21 years later.

An unusual vehicle in the fleet of Great Yarmouth Corporation is their No.42, a new Leyland Atlantean with 39-seat Marshall single-deck bodywork, one of three recently delivered.

In total contrast, Great Yarmouth EX5264 is a wartime utility Guy Arab I, now used by the Corporation as a travelling library. It has Strachans 56-seat bodywork and was new in 1944 as their No.17.

On a wet and dismal 23 March 1968, Keighley West Yorkshire 1966 Bristol FS6B 60-seat Lodekka KDX225 stands outside Keighley Station.

An OTC visit on 28 April 1968 to West Bridgford Urban District Council's depot finds their No.31, an AEC Regent V with unusual Reading 59-seat lowbridge bodywork, one of three new in 1958.

A one-off vehicle in this fleet is No.21, an AEC Regent III with Willowbrook 55-seat lowbridge bodywork, new in 1954.

Bearing Park Royal highbridge 60-seat bodywork, No.23 is one of four AEC Regent IIIs so-bodied for the UDC in 1948.

Similar-looking No.3 is also a Regent III, but with 56-seat Park Royal bodywork, one of two new in 1947.

Illustrating how West Bridgford kept faith with AEC, No.43 is a new Swift with East Lancs 46-seat bodywork, new in September 1967. It was their last new vehicle, as the fleet was taken over by Nottingham City Transport the following year.

We also visited Nottingham independent operator Skills that day. Their No.60 (FRC951) is an all-Leyland Titan PD2/12 58-seater, new to Trent Motor Traction as their No.741 in 1955.

We visited Barton, too. At their Ilkeston depot, several ex-London Transport Leyland PD2s of the RTL class (and a solitary RTW) were based. Of this group, No.1110 (MXX34) had been LT's RTL1335 and, curiously, took a trip to Czechoslovakia in 1966, but returned to LT for a few months' more service before withdrawal in 1967.

In Epsom on 28 May 1968 for the Derby is pre-war ECW-bodied 56-seat Bristol K5G CAP205, new in 1940 to Brighton, Hove & District (BH&D) as their No.6351. It was rebuilt as a convertible open-topper in 1951, retaining its original body, and then sold to Thomas Brothers of Port Talbot in 1960 and named *Afan Belle*. After withdrawal it was exported to Canada.

A visit to a rather wintry Brighton on 29 March 1969 finds the Brighton, Hove & District fleet now taken over by Southdown, but for the time being still in their old liveries and carrying BH&D fleet numbers. No.9 is a Bristol FS6B Lodekka, new for the 1960 season with ECW convertible open-top 60-seat bodywork, seen heading north from Old Steine bound for Hollingbury. Such vehicles had all-cream livery, rather than the usual red and cream.

Seen turning off Lewes Road on route 43 bound for Race Hill, ECW-bodied Bristol RESL6G dual-door 35-seater No.206 is one of the last vehicles delivered to BH&D in July 1968 before its takeover by Southdown.

At the same location, and typifying BH&D vehicles built in the 1950s, No.460 is a 1954 60-seat ECW-bodied Bristol KSW6G seen heading into town on route 54. For several years, such routes had been pooled between Southdown, BH&D and Brighton Corporation, the latter having a virtually identical livery to BH&D.

Showing how nicely the red and cream BH&D livery suited Bristol Lodekkas, 1962 60-seat FS6B XPM49 heads for Hove when seen at Old Steine.

Brighton, Hove & District still purchased Bristol K-types as late as 1957, having some of the last to be built. Here, No.485, a standard 60-seat KSW6G new in 1956, is about to be overtaken by 1967 FLF6G 70-seater No.92 in St James Street. Both are passing *The Bulldog*, a pub I was to get to know very well in the 1990s.

ABOUT THE AUTHOR

Jim Blake was born at the end of 1947, just five days before the 'Big Four' railway companies and many bus companies – including London Transport – were nationalised by Clement Attlee's Labour government.

Like most young lads born in the early post-war years, he soon developed a passionate interest in railways, in particular the myriad steam engines still running on Britain's railways in those days. However, because his home in Canonbury Avenue, Islington, was just a few minutes' walk from North London's last two tram routes, the 33 in Essex Road and the 35 in Holloway Road and Upper Street, Jim's parents often took him on these for outings to the South Bank, particularly to the Festival of Britain which was held there in the last summer they ran, in 1951. Moreover, Jim's father worked at the GPO's West Central District Office in Holborn and often travelled to and from work on the 35 tram. As a result, he knew many of the tram crews, who would let Jim stand by the driver at the front of the trams as they travelled through the Kingsway Tram Subway. This was an unforgettable experience for a four-year-old! In addition, Jim's home was in the heart of North London's trolleybus system, with route 611 actually passing his home, and one of the busiest and complicated trolleybus junctions in the world, Holloway Nag's Head, a short ride away along Holloway Road. Here, the trolleybuses' overhead wires almost blotted out the sky! Thus from a very early age, Jim developed an equal interest in buses and trolleybuses to that in railways, and has retained both until the present day.

Jim was educated at his local Highbury County Grammar School, and later at Kingsway College, by coincidence a stone's throw from the old tram subway. He was first bought a camera for his 14th birthday at the end of 1961, which was immediately put to good use photographing the last London trolleybuses in North West London on their very snowy last day a week later. Three years later, he started work as an administrator for the old London County Council at County Hall, by coincidence adjacent to the former Festival of Britain site, and travelled to and from work on bus routes 171 or 172, which had replaced the 33 and 35 trams mentioned above!

By now, Jim's interest in buses and trolleybuses had expanded to include those of other operators, and he travelled throughout England and Wales between 1961 and 1968 in pursuit of them, being able to afford to travel further afield after starting work! He also bought a colour cine-camera in 1965, with which he was able to capture what is now very rare footage of long-lost buses, trolleybuses and steam locomotives. Where the latter are concerned, he was one of the initial purchasers of the unique British Railways 'Pacific' locomotive 71000 *Duke of Gloucester*, which was the last ever passenger express steam engine built for use in Britain. Other preservationists laughed at the group which purchased what in effect was a cannibalised hulk from Barry